CW00569960

CONTENTS

Clean Less Play More:

Housekeeping for Normal People

Stephanie O'Dea

Disclaimer

While best efforts have been used, the author is not offering legal, accounting, medical, or any other professional services advice and makes no representations or warranties of any kind and assumes no liabilities of any kind with respect to the accuracy or completeness of the contents.

The author shall not be held liable or responsible to any person or entity with respect to any loss or incidental or consequential damages caused, or alleged to have been caused, directly or indirectly, by the information contained herein.

This book contains affiliate links which means that if a purchase is made through the provided link, the author may receive a portion of the sale.

Although all attempts have been made to verify the information provided in this book, the author does not assume any responsibility for errors, omissions, or contrary interpretations of the subject matter.

The views expressed are those of the author alone, and should not be taken as expert instruction or commands. The reader is responsible for his or her own actions. Adherence to all applicable laws and regulations, including international, federal, state, and local governing professional licensing, business practices, advertising, and all other aspects of doing business in the United States or any other jurisdiction is the sole responsibility of the purchaser or reader.

ISBN: 9798668818662

INTRODUCTION

The Back Story

I like things clean.

but I don't really *like* cleaning.

I notice that our family runs more smoothly when there is order and stability in our home. The kids are better behaved when their living space is organized and they know where their things belong.

I love being able to spontaneously invite friends over without fear of dirty dishes crowding the kitchen sink, wet towels on the bathroom floor, or messy unmade beds.

I like being able to shrug when the kids lick crumbs from the floor (will the playing-cat-game ever get old?).

I like that we can plan outings on the weekend rather than spend valuable free time cleaning up after a way-too-busy week.

I like that the laundry is manageable and not overwhelming.

But I still don't *like* cleaning.

Instead, I prefer to do a little bit every day (or have someone else do it!) so I never spend a whole entire day inside cleaning when I could be outside having fun!

I have chosen to Clean Less and Play More.

How This Book Came to Be

Thank you for being here and for taking the time to read through this book. I first began working on it roughly 18 years ago, when my oldest was still a baby. She is now off to college and I figure I might as well finish what I started way back then!

I wanted to write this book because as a young wife and mother, I was frazzled and overwhelmed. I wanted the "Martha Stewart" type of household -- (remember, this was WAY before Pinterest and Instagram!) -- but truth be told, I am actually a rather lazy person.

I wanted the biggest bang for the least amount of effort. That is how I came up with "The Daily 7" which has since been written about in my *Totally Together: Shortcuts to an Organized Life* book and journal.

This book, or at least *the idea* for this book, came about at the same time.

There are a few things to keep in mind when Cleaning Less and Playing More:

- if it isn't dirty, don't clean it
- if you do a little bit every day, it won't get overwhelming
- if you get it out, put it away
- you are in charge of your own stuff
- help each other
- children learn by example
- don't expect your home to look like a magazine spread. This is real life
- if you have too much stuff, it's time to P.R.O.M. (acronym explained later)
- don't bring stuff home unless you know where it's going to go
- changing habits takes time

The beauty of the Clean Less, Play More methodology is how easy it is to get back on track when Real Life happens.

If you take or have to take the day off, you can rest easy knowing that your home isn't going to get horribly out of hand because it's tended to regularly.

I promise that once you get a hold of the daily, weekly, monthly, and sporadic chores, you'll have much more time to do the things you want to do. You'll have the time to update the scrapbooks, do crafts, read fun-for-you books, spend time with the kids, and sleep.

mmm. Sleep.

A Clean Home is Better
For Your Health

Anyone who suffers from allergies to dust or mold can tell you that the best way to feel better is to keep your inside living space as clean as possible.

A clean home leaves fewer places for germs and bacteria to hide. Plus, dust and allergens build up in carpeting, bedding and upholstery over time, which can exacerbate existing allergies and asthma.

A clean and organized home is also very good for your mental and emotional state. In my *How To Live Slowly* book, I talk about how people who are emotionally healthy are in control of their thoughts, feelings, and behaviors. They are able to cope with life's challenges. They can keep problems in perspective and bounce back from setbacks.

Keeping a tidy house can be overwhelming if there is too much stuff to clean, organize, and maintain. I will teach you my simple method of decluttering later on in this book. The less stuff you have in your home, the easier it is to keep it clean.

Cleaning can be therapeutic to many. Some psychologists proclaim that maintaining a clean and organized home can produce a sense of accomplishment, happiness, serenity, and clarity.

Courtney Lopresti, M.S., has a background in neuroscience. She writes in *Psychology Today*, "our bodies are organized systems designed to self-clean. It wouldn't be surprising, then, if the reason we crave symmetry and cleanliness in our homes is to mirror the organization within our very own bodies." She also proclaims,"Neatness and order support health — and oppose chaos."

MENTAL HEALTH BENEFITS
OF A CLEAN HOUSE

1. DE-STRESSING

A 2009 study led by associate professor NiCole R. Keith, Ph.D., research scientist and professor at Indiana University, found that women with high levels of cortisol, a stress-indicating hormone, revealed to doctors through a survey that their houses were disorganized and cluttered.

On the flip side, women who self-reported they were more comfortable and happy had more organized houses. This de-stressing is also correlated with a healthier body—eating more nutritious foods, getting better sleep, building your immune system, and being more active.

2. MINDFULNESS

The mindlessness of cleaning allows you to practice mindfulness and meditation. Cleaning, it turns out, can help you live in the present and practice focusing. The *Wall Street Journal* reported in May 2020 that those who deem household chores in a meditative light do not look at cleaning as a chore, but rather look forward to washing a sink full of dishes.

3. INCREASING PRODUCTIVITY

A more organized and clean house can lead to more production, according to the Princeton Neuroscience Institute in 2001.

You're less stressed and more focused without distractions from clutter and dirt. Without distraction, your mind can process at a faster pace.

4. ENSURING SOCIAL CONFIDENCE

If you're having friends, family, or even casual acquaintances into your living space, it can be anxiety-inducing if you don't have a clean house. In today's Instagram and HGTV saturated society, it's easy for people to feel as if their home doesn't measure up. Confidence in your own house's cleanliness when entertaining can help alleviate feelings of inadequacy.

We can't all have gourmet kitchens and barn doors sectioning off the dining room, but we certainly can keep dust bunnies away!

5. SPARKING CREATIVITY

A kept house can spark creativity. Maybe you'll innovate your storage, think of new decor ideas, and envision a whole new furniture layout just by being able to see what's there (and what isn't)! Some of my readers have even started side hustles by selling unneeded books, craft supplies, or baby toys on ebay or etsy.

6. REDUCING FAMILIAL FIGHTING

Not being able to find a soccer cleat right before the big game, or misplacing a utility bill is very stressful and can lead to bickering and accusations. When everything in your home has a place, and all family members agree to maintain order, you will have a lot less tension in your home.

7. WARDS OFF PROCRASTINATION

When you have a task you don't want to start, do you ever find yourself scanning the room for a distraction? Disorganization makes it easy to spot something you can use to procrastinate. When everything is in order, on the other hand, your mind finds it easier to get stuff done.

8. YOU MIGHT EAT HEALTHIER

Have you ever noticed that when you're feeling stressed, you crave junk food or something with sugar? This is your body's natural response to stressors and – as previously mentioned – clutter and messiness are stressful.

There is good news, though: cleaning and organizing doesn't just make you less likely to want food that's bad for you, it can actually help drive healthy choices.

A 2016 research study by Cornell called *Clutter, Chaos, and Overconsumption* presented people with food choices. Those who worked in an organized space were two times more likely to choose an apple over a chocolate bar than those who had been working in a messy area.

Pretty interesting!

LET'S GET STARTED!

I don't clean much. I never spend a day cleaning. There are heaps of things more fun than cleaning that my family and I would rather do. Reading, playing games, doing puzzles, watching TV, gardening, exercising and even flossing all beat out my desire to clean.

That said, my family and I enjoy an orderly lifestyle and as an added bonus we find that we all get along better when our home is tidy and we follow a routine.

This leads to comfort and happiness for all of us -- the dog, included!

In order to balance our desire for structure and our displeasure for cleaning, our family has learned to Clean Less and Play More.

Together, we have discovered the key to having more family fun -- I know it sounds simplistic, bear with me.

The plan is to do a little bit of work each day, rather than putting all cleaning off to the weekend and risk ruining precious days of togetherness.

To keep our home in order, our family has a list of chores we do daily, rain or shine. These chores are easy to remember and can be accomplished by any member of the family (yes, even the children can help).

To get our system running smoothly, I needed to tweak our definition of "clean." We adopted highly realistic in-home goals.

I no longer wish for our home to resemble the sterile environments depicted in home design magazines, Pinterest, or on HGTV. Instead, I want our family home to be tidy and comfortable and to reflect each person who lives in it.

Company Coming?

If our family is expecting company, I only take the time to put out clean guest towels and prepare food. I vacuum (or delegate it) *after* our visitors leave.

There is no mad dash to "crash clean" because the house is always in good order. The children may have to put away a few stray shoes or toys, but our house is always company-ready.

Real Life

The beauty of the Clean Less, Play More (CLPM) system is how easy it is to get back on track when you take, or have to take, a day off.

Children get sick, toilets break, keys get locked into cars, the washing machine floods, etc. Life and all it's obstacles can wreak havoc on even the best-planned days.

The best thing you can do is to go with the flow and get back on track the next day. When bathrooms are attended to regularly, they will not become scummy or mildew-infested when a day simply doesn't allow a wipe down.

There is only one thing to remember when learning how to Clean Less and Play More. This will sound too easy:

IF IT'S NOT DIRTY, DON'T CLEAN IT.

Do not waste precious time cleaning something that is already clean. Many of the things we spend the most time scrubbing are actually pretty clean already.

Toilets, showers, sinks, dishwashers and tubs are essentially self-cleaning. They need a bit of help to keep them gleaming and sanitized, but they really don't need to be scoured weekly or even monthly if they are cared for properly and dirt and grime aren't allowed to congregate.

I will share cleaning shortcuts and a task time-line so you, too, do not waste valued energy over-cleaning.

Spot Clean

An important way to save treasured family time is by learning how to spot-clean. If there is a spot of toothpaste on the bathroom mirror, there is no need to spray the entire mirror with cleanser.

If your child spills cereal on the floor, sweep up the immediate area. Don't roll up your sleeves and wax the linoleum.

Do not over-work. This is not a competition. No prizes will be handed out for the extra energy and time you spent cleaning house.

When spot cleaning becomes a habit, you will be well on your way to a happy and harmonious household.

There are seven key chores that need to be accomplished daily to keep your home running smoothly and to promote tranquility. These daily tasks can be done by anyone in the family. Feel free to delegate to your spouse and children.

This is the *family's* home and these are the *family's* chores.

It will take some time to commit these daily tasks to memory and for them to become second nature.

Are you ready? Let's get started!

THE DAILY 7 FOR A
HIGHLY SUCCESSFUL
HOUSEHOLD

I adore the Stephen Covey Books. I love the way that he breaks down complex ideas into seven easy steps. While I was implementing our daily family chores, I thought limiting it to Covey's "7" seemed like a good idea.

This way there are enough chores to get things accomplished, but not too many to feel overwhelming. These seven daily tasks can be done by anyone in the family and will keep your home running smoothly and promote tranquility.

We're still real people, and we don't live in a museum. I'm not going to lead you astray and say that I make sure the following tasks occur each and every day no matter what. I might burst into flames.

Our house isn't spotless. It isn't pristine. But it is clean.

I look at it as getting all the Have-Tos over and Done With so there is more time in the day for the Want-Tos.

And trust me. Cleaning never has been nor it ever will be a WANT TO!

Here is the list -- the idea is to do them every day, rain or shine.

Number 1: Make Beds Right Away

Number 2: Do One Complete Load of Laundry

Number 3: Empty All Garbage Cans

Number 4: Keep Your Kitchen Sink Empty

Number 5: Clean Up After Yourself and Help Children Do the Same

Number 6: Bathroom Wipe-Down

Number 7: Before Bed 10-Minute Clean Up

The Daily 7 -- In More Detail

Number 1: Make Beds Right Away

As soon as you rise in the morning, make your bed. Help or remind your children to do the same. This is a wonderful habit to get into. The sense of accomplishment that comes from seeing a made bed is enough to carry many people through the entire morning.

"It's only 6:30 and I've already *done* something!"

Simplify

Streamline the bed linen in your home. Invest in quality comforters with washable covers. That way, even the youngest toddler can feel the satisfaction of making his own bed.
All they need to do is pull up the sheet and straighten the comforter. Extra blankets can be folded and stored at the foot of the bed.

Get rid of the decorative pillows. Fuzzy-squeezies don't serve a purpose other than to provide a cozy home for dust mites. Too much time and energy is spent fluffing and arranging.

While you are tossing unnecessary items, get rid of dust ruffles. Not only are they difficult to clean, they never hang right and they frequently get tucked under the mattress during bed making.

In general, they serve no purpose other than to cause frustration. Dust ruffles also tend to give the impression that it is okay to shove things haphazardly under the bed.

It is not.

Number 2: Do One Complete Load of Laundry

Laundry is a hassle. It piles up, it finds a dark corner in which to multiply, and it never goes away.

Ever.

Finish a complete load of laundry every day. A "complete load" means it has been washed, dried, folded and put away.

It doesn't matter if this is a full load or not. Just complete the task.

The CLPM methodology is easily applied to laundry. If you don't have to wash it, don't. If you don't have to separate colors, don't.

Assign each household member a bath towel to use for the entire week. Hang the towels to dry between showers and baths.

Unless you have severe allergies in your family, you only need to change bed linens every other week.

Laundry & Kids

Keep track of how long your children wear their clothes during the day. When my children were five, they enjoyed changing clothes a few times a day.

Clothes that are changed hourly do not need to be laundered.

If you change your clothes when you get home from work, consider using the same at-home clothes each day. If they have only been worn for a few hours while sitting on the couch watching TV, they are more than likely just fine to wear again.

More tips:

- Place dirty socks in a lingerie bag to keep pairs together
- Wash colored clothing inside out to preserve brightness
- Pre-treat all stains as soon as you notice them occurring
- Prevent stains by using aprons, bibs or by wearing dark clothing (I have been known to strip my children down to their undies as they eat spaghetti)
- Don't wash large items (such as pillows or sleeping bags) in your own washing machine. Wash them instead at a laundromat.
- Very young children can learn to sort dark and light clothing and to match socks.
- Beginning at age 18 months, children can help put away

their own clothes into dresser drawers.

My friend, Liz, has five young children in her home. She shared that she purchases white athletic socks for all of the kids. Since socks span a wide range of sizes, her children all grab from the same stash in the morning, easing both laundry-folding and the morning dressing routine.

If this isn't a possibility for you in your household, consider giving each of your children a mesh "lingerie" bag for their socks. This way they are already pre-bundled for washing and can easily be matched. This trick also helps with missing sock problems!

Number 3: Empty all Garbage Cans

This one is pretty self-explanatory. Empty all wastebaskets and garbage cans at least once a day, perhaps after dinner.

If you have stinky items to throw away (such as poopy diapers or tuna fish cans) take them immediately to the outdoor garbage or recycle bin. This will help eliminate any offensive odors in your home.

Small children can help with this task by gathering the smaller wastebaskets throughout the house and emptying them into a large bag to be taken out.

Make sure that the recyclables are also taken out daily.

Pro Tip:

Put a fabric softener sheet under the plastic can liner to ward off icky smells.

Number 4: Keep Your Kitchen Sink Empty

The fourth habit to include in your daily routine is to keep your kitchen sink empty.

This means that when you finish using a plate or utensil, either put the item directly into the dishwasher, or wash it by hand.

If dishes are allowed to rest in the sink, other pieces of flatware are mysteriously attracted, and before long the sink is rendered useless.
Do not let this happen!

While preparing meals or cooking, wash pots and pans while you go along or immediately stack them into the dishwasher. Clear and clean the dinner dishes as soon as possible.

If you absolutely must soak a pot or casserole dish, set a timer so you won't forget to retrieve it from the sink.

Go to bed each night with an empty sink. There are few things as discouraging as being greeted in the morning by last night's dirty dishes.

Enlist Help

When I operated the child-care facility at a homeless shelter, children in my care were urged to clear their own place setting at age 18 months. Young children love washing dishes.

Pull up a chair and fill the sink with warm sudsy water. Your dishes and your child's grubby fingernails will be washed together.

When entertaining, say "yes" to the help offered by your guests.

Your friends will gladly assist in clearing the dinner table and stacking the dishwasher. They will also leave feeling helpful and useful, feelings that we all enjoy.

Number 5: Clean Up After Yourself and Help Children Do the Same

This sounds so simple, doesn't it? This is the most important chore to incorporate into your family's daily routine.

- If you take it out, put it away.
- If you spill it, wipe it up.
- If you knock it over, pick it up.
- If you open it, close it.
- If you make it cry, say you're sorry and give it a hug.

(So, maybe the last one doesn't pertain to housekeeping, but it's a good all-around rule to follow.)

I am not suggesting that you spend your day policing your family's every action, but each family member really should be responsible for his or her own mess.

Help small children with this by encouraging them to put away one toy before bringing out another.

Schedule impromptu "Pick-Ups" throughout the day and before meals and bed times. Monitor your children in the kitchen and remind them that it is their responsibility to sweep up crumbs left under their dining chair.

Ten Minute Tidy

Set the microwave timer for 10 minutes, or tell Alexa or Siri to start a timer for you. Hand your child an empty laundry basket. Put stray toys, clothing, shoes and other items into basket.

Have children race to beat the clock while returning items to their rightful home.

Schedule these 10 Minute Tidies throughout the day -- especially on a weekend or summer day when everybody is at home.

If you've got a family of five, and they each work for 10 minutes, that is an AWFUL LOT of cleaning that gets accomplished!

Elsa Is Wrong.

When it comes to daily cleaning and keeping an organized and tranquil home, Elsa is wrong. The best thing you can do is to NOT let it go.

Instead, if you see it, pick it up.

Do not walk over the stranded *GI Joe* in the middle of the living room. Pick him up and return him to his comrades, or ask his owner to do it.

Do not ignore the *Cheerio* under the kitchen table. Pick it up before it is stepped on and the crumbs are tracked throughout the home.

If you notice a smudge on the light switch, wipe it off. Tackle things that you notice immediately, before they get any worse or before you get side-tracked.

Keep kid-safe and kid-sized cleaning products accessible. A brightly colored dust-pan and hand-broom set will be used more often when a child knows where it lives.

Leave packages of baby wipes within reach to entice your child to wipe up their own sticky spills.

Number 6: Bathroom Wipe-Down

The next chore on your daily list is a complete bathroom wipe-down. This really isn't as odious as it sounds. You need to begin with an already clean bathroom. Clean your bathroom the way you normally would, and then you can proceed with the daily maintenance.

30 Minute or Less Highly Efficient Bathroom Clean-Up

Remove bathmats. Put stray items into cabinets. Clear counter-tops completely. Sweep or vacuum flooring.

Spray the mirror, sink, countertop, and all fixtures with an all-surface bathroom cleanser. If you have other bathrooms in the home—attend to them in the same way while the cleanser sits in the first.

Go back to the first bathroom and starting with the mirror, wipe all surfaces with a dry cloth. It will become damp. Wipe the outside of the toilet with your cloth, but use lengths of toilet paper to wipe out the inner lid, seat, rim and bowl. Flush away the used paper as needed.

Toilet paper is inexpensive, use it!

Use your damp cloth to wipe up the flooring. Continue on to the other bathrooms.

When finished, toss soiled cloth into the washing machine.

Now that the Bathroom is Clean -- this is how you keep it that way:

Once each day, quickly wipe down all surfaces in the bathroom. A good time to do this is after a bath or shower, when there are still water puddles.

Grab an item from the dirty clothes pile (t-shirts work great) and use it to dry shower doors or ledges of the tub.
This will help keep mold and soap-scum from adhering. Many people leave a squeegee in the shower to remove moisture from the door and enclosure.

Take another clothing item from your dirty clothes pile to wipe down the sink and countertop. Polish the faucets and rinse away any stray toothpaste from the basin.
When finished, spot clean the mirror to remove any toothpaste speckles.

Use the damp clothing item to wipe up the floor. This will keep dust from congregating and help ease future floor scrubbing.

Bathtime Supervision = Cleaning Time

When my children were younger, they each took an evening bath, which resulted in water splashed on the floor.

I got into the habit of simply using the towel I used on the floor to collect the spills and splashes to quickly wipe down the entire bathroom while I was also keeping an eye on them.

It worked well, the kids were happy, and in turn I had a sparkling bathroom which made me happy, too!

The Toilet

Toilets are essentially self-cleaning, yet most of us are completely disgusted at the thought of cleaning them. To maintain a sparkling toilet, wipe or swish it out daily.

Use a disinfectant wipe to clean the entire outside of the toilet before moving to the inside.

Clean your toilet with the wipe in this order:

- top side of lid
- top and sides of water tank
- inner lid
- seat
- underside of toilet seat
- rim
- bowl

Many wipes can not be flushed. Be sure to read the manufacturer's instructions for proper disposal.

Pull on some utility gloves and wipe out the inside of the toilet with toilet paper. If you cannot fathom the thought of immersing your hand (or even part of your hand) into the toilet, use a toilet brush.

Please make sure that the toilet brush is stored out of reach of young, inquisitive fingers. Toilet brush holders, even a decorative one, are kind of gross and don't really keep the germs away.

Keep Your Toilet Lid Down

It is good feng-shui, safer for children, more sanitary, and it just looks nicer.

If you ever want to ick yourself out, try googling "germs in air after flushing a toilet" -- it's pretty disgusting, but keeping the lid down helps to alleviate this problem!

Number 7: Before Bed Tidy-Up

Remember the nice feeling of awakening in the morning to clean dishes and an empty kitchen sink? Spread the joy throughout the house by insisting on a quick tidy-up routine before retiring for the night.

Instruct family members to police the living spaces for stray items. Put shoes away, file the mail appropriately, straighten the couch cushions and push in the dining room chairs.

Have children return toys to their rightful places. Before bed is a perfect time to schedule a 10 Minute Tidy as described in number 5.

How to Keep Mail and Paper from Piling Up

Do not collect your mail until you are prepared to deal with it. Sort incoming mail near the garbage can. Toss all un-needed envelopes, junk mail and advertising circulars.

As soon as it's feasibly convenient, RSVP to events and mark the times, dates, and locations on your calendar.

This quick 10-15 minute tidy-up routine will ensure a restful (or at least a bit more restful!) night's sleep. You can start the day without being annoyed by yesterday's messes.

When the "Daily 7" are included in your everyday routine, they become so second nature that you no longer need to think about them.

Instinctively picking up around the home will become as automatic as brushing your teeth before heading to bed for the night.

WEEKLY/MONTHLY/ SEASONAL CHORES (AKA: ALL THE OTHER STUFF)

A Task Time Line

T ask times do not have to be tedious -- I get most of my cleaning done in bits and spurts throughout the day. I rarely schedule cleaning but instead choose to clean on an as-needed basis. I have found, however, that patterns have emerged to show how often certain household tasks usually need to be completed.

This list is to be used as a guideline - only a guideline. You are still the boss.

Once A Week

- vacuum flooring

Although some vacuum manufacturers advise against it, I vacuum all the flooring in our house—-including bathrooms, and the garage!

Vacuuming captures a lot of fly-around dust and lint. Be sure to put the vacuum onto the setting without the revolving beater bar if you are not using it to vacuum carpeting.

Keep a 30-foot extension cord with your vacuum cleaner so you don't need to change outlets as you go through the house.

- mop kitchen

Quick Mopping Method

After removing surface bits, spray glass cleanser directly onto the floor. Run hot water in the kitchen sink. Wet mop head thoroughly and mop as you normally would. Rinse

Clear off kitchen counter, spray with glass cleanser and wipe with sponge

- wipe out microwave
- replace sponge
- dust house

Easy Microwave Cleaning:

You can sterilize a damp sponge by microwaving it and letting it cook on high for thirty seconds. Then use it to wipe down the walls, inner door and floor of the microwave.

How to Speed Dust

I like microfiber dusting cloths. I like the way they trap dust. They don't spread it all around like dry dusting with a towel, or fluff it into the air like a feather duster.

If you don't have microfiber cloths, find a stack of old rags, t-shirts, cloth diapers, or socks without mates. Mist your cloth lightly with glass cleanser (you can use water or a vinegar solution if you prefer) and wipe your way around the room as fast as you can.

Tackle all horizontal surfaces working your way from highest to lowest.

Move in a clockwise manner until the room is finished. Do not get compulsive about dusting every little knick-knack perfectly. Pick it up, wipe quickly and wipe the spot it was in. Then move on.

Only spend a few minutes in each room---speed is the name of the game. Chuck out used rags or toss them into the washing machine for future use.

Twice A Month

- toothpick clean

[Use the pointy end of a toothpick to scrape out gunk that collects in cracks of kitchen appliances and faucet bases.]

- change bedding
- bathroom deep clean

Once A Month

- dust blinds

[an easy way to dust blinds, is to put an old sock onto each hand]

- sweep or hose off front porch
- polish furniture
- clean out car

About the Car...

I have a messy car. It pretty much resembles a closet and playpen on wheels. I've tried to clean it weekly, daily and after each use.

So far, nothing has worked as well as the motivation of picking my mom up once a month for a shopping date.

Do what works best for your family.

Quarterly

- wipe off the top of the refrigerator, the door, and inner shelving
- wash outside of cabinet doors in the kitchen
- clean finger and nose prints off windows

Twice A Year

- change smoke detector batteries
- hose off outside of house and windows
- flip mattresses
- change HVAC filters

Schedule these twice a year chores to correspond with Daylight Savings time to help jog your memory.

MUST-HAVE CLEANING SUPPLIES

Equipment

<u>Broom:</u> Have an indoor broom, and another for outside. An angled edge makes it easier to get under kitchen cabinets.

<u>Dustpan and Hand Broom Set:</u> Child- sized tools lure children into cleaning up after themselves.

<u>Mop:</u> I like steam mops that have a cloth cover I can throw into the laundry, but you can also use Swiffer or easy mopping systems that use either disposable or washable cloths.

Don't buy a sponge or fabric mop that isn't easy for you to keep clean -- it doesn't make sense to mop your flooring with an already dirty mop!

Dustmop: If you have hardwood flooring, this is a mop that is used to keep it shiny and to keep lint and dust from accumulating. No water is used. You can use the kind that take disposable cloths (Swiffer or the like), or one with fitted removable pads that you launder and re-use.

Vacuum: Choose an upright bagless vacuum and empty it into the outside garbage can after each use.

Dust Rags: I like microfiber fabric for dusting because the dust is trapped instantly and is easily laundered. Old towels, torn T-shirts, cloth diapers, and holey socks also make excellent dust rags. If you'd like your children to dust, it might be useful to use baby wipes because then the dust gets trapped in the moisture rather than getting shoved around.

Toothpicks: These are quite handy for cleaning crevices around the edges of sinks, faucets, and the stove. I like to wrap a disinfecting wipe around the pointy edge of a toothpick and clean crevices while chatting on the phone.

HOW TO EFFECTIVELY DE-CLUTTER

T he less you have, the easier it is to keep your home clean. This is a fact.

You don't need to become a minimalist, but you do need to be able to find a happy balance between owning stuff without feeling like your stuff owns you.

You will also find that when you own less stuff you will physically feel freer and lighter and feel fulfilled by the stuff you already own.

Have you ever heard the phrase "Life is what happens while you are busy making other plans"

What about, "Life is what happens while you're busy buying stuff, maintaining your stuff and working to buy more stuff?"

In my *How to Live Slowly* book, I write about how one of the best ways to keep yourself positive is to live in the moment and take the time to truly value all that is around you. I shared that my children have a sign hanging in their bathroom that I found in the clearance section at Marshall's -- it reads: It is Not Happy People Who are Thankful, but Thankful People Who are Happy.

Make time for things you enjoy, and try your hardest to focus on positive things in your life. This is much easier if you aren't wasting time digging through your closet to find the other tennis shoe or wading through piles of papers to find a needed receipt.

It's P.R.O.M. Time!

Don't worry, I'm not suggesting that you don a strapless turquoise gown covered in sequins. Today's PROM is not an over-priced school dance but an acronym for an efficient way to de-clutter: Purge, Remove, Organize, Maintain.

After you have established the *Daily 7 for a Highly Successful Household*, it's time to tackle the hidden unk lurking in the closets, garages, attics, dresser drawers, and under beds.

stephanieodea.com

NOT a dance, but a
decluttering method!

Give me a P!

The "P" in PROM is for purge.

Grab a garbage can or large plastic sack and get moving. When faced with a de-cluttering challenge, enter a room and quickly toss all items that are obviously garbage.

Move as fast as you can, and try not to over-think your decisions.

One *Barbie* shoe? Toss it.

Last year's invite to your third-cousin's fourth son's baptism party that you didn't go to but the picture on the card reminds you of when your now-nine-year-old used to listen? Toss it.

Once you have filled your bin or your sack, put the lid on or tie it up.

The next pass through the room (or drawer, box, bookshelf, etc.) will not be so easy. With another box or bin, assess the remaining items. Try to keep this simple.

- If you don't need it, toss it.

- If you can't remember what it is, toss it.

- If you don't know the last time you used it, but you think you might need it someday in the future but you don't know when that will be, toss it.

Release the clutter and reclaim your home. The less "stuff" you have, the less you have to clean.

Give Me an R!

The "R" in PROM stands for the word "remove."

Get rid of your purged things quickly. Do not have a second look at your purged items, and most certainly, don't let the bags of purged items sit around long enough for children to rifle through and discover lost treasure.

Take the garbage out to the outdoor can or take a trip to the dump.

Donate still-useful items to charity. There are numerous charities listed in your local phone book, which would greatly benefit from your cast-offs. Many will come to your home for a pick-up, and they all offer tax-deduction receipts.

If you and your family would rather hold a garage sale, schedule it as soon as possible. Holding on to a pile of purged stuff to sell is almost as bad as if you never purged in the first place. Sell quickly and arrange for a charity pick-up to collect all remaining items.

Give Me an O!

"O" is for "organize."

Take the time to organize the remaining items in your newly de-cluttered space. Put like items together and use baskets or plastic bins to contain small items. Storage containers do not need to be expensive.

In our house, many of the bins we use to store toys, games, or clothing accessories came from the dollar store. Depending on space, consider installing extra shelves, hooks, or a pegboard to help maintain order.

If you find that you continue to have more items than available storage space, purge again with a more discerning eye.

I know it's tough to get rid of things, but remember that it's the *people* that count in your house, not the *things*.

Give Me an M!

The last step is "M", "maintain."

Spend time on a daily basis putting things back where they belong. Take a photo of your hard work and hang it in the newly de-cluttered environment to remind children (and spouses!) what the space *should* and *can* look like with just a touch of effort.

Explain that it is everyone's responsibility, not just yours, to help ensure cleanliness and order.

Give yourself a pat on the back. Your children deserve to live in a de-cluttered, calm, and peaceful home. You deserve it too.

CREATE A PUNCH LIST

G rowing up, I constantly heard the term "punch list," because my dad was an architect. After college, I married a Civil Engineer, so I STILL hear the term an awful lot!

Punch Lists have always been a way of life for me.

When I started writing daily on the Internet, I learned that not everybody was familiar with the concept of creating a running punch list, and the term is not as well known to a lot of people.

No problem!

It's really not a big deal — a Punch List simply means the stuff left on your To Do List before the job is considered "Finished."

And our homes?

They are constantly ebbing and flowing and in constant I-Need-Attention mode.

It doesn't matter if you rent or own or if you live in a Tiny House, a farmhouse, a high rise apartment, or a nice suburban family home. -- there is always STUFF that needs fixing or repairing or mending.

And that's the stuff to put onto your punch list!

The easiest way to get started with creating an ongoing punch list is to get out a spiral notebook or put a few sheets of lined paper onto a clipboard.

Then walk through every room in the house.

Jot down everything that needs to be done to get your house in good repair, or the stuff that has been bugging you.

Do the baseboards need to be painted? Pictures hung? Light bulbs changed? Drywall patched?

Also jot down notes as to any upgrades you may want to do. Are you thinking that you want/need a new chair for the living room? A better or different light fixture in the front entry?

Write those down too.

The next step is to separate your list into separate rooms. Put all the garden things together, the kid stuff together, etc. I like to make a sheet of paper per room —

(the reason we didn't start with separate sheets to begin with is because sometimes if you see a light fixture in one room that needs fixing, etc., you start writing down things in a ping-pong fashion — and that's okay!)

Now that all your items are separated by rooms, separate them again by what you can truly and physically do yourself.

If you can hang a photo on the wall in the hallway, then do it.

If you can touch up the paint, then schedule a time to do it.

Do as much as you can all by yourself before calling in help from a handyman or outside help.

Keep your Punch List up to date and organized the best you can. If Lawn Furniture was on sale and you bought it, cross it off your list.

Once your home is decluttered and in good order, you can start doing some of the "grander" projects like repainting the dining room or ripping out the back lawn.

BUT THAT'S WHY
WE HAD YOU!

*Children make messes. It's
part of their job.*

Before I had children of my own, I ran preschool centers for under-privileged children, and one of the sites was in a transitional housing facility.

Because I was able to get a classroom of twenty-four toddlers and pre-schoolers to tidy up their messes, I was pretty sure that when I had children of my own it would be a piece of cake getting them to clean up after themselves.

I was dead wrong.

It takes daily effort to remind my children to put their clothing, toys, and personal paraphernalia away. That's just how it works.

Although your children will probably never stop needing your helpful reminders, even the youngest child can quickly learn that being part of a family means helping to care for the family home. Performing household chores promotes responsibility, independence and commitment.

Children naturally want to help their parents. Many children love to play house and will spend hours setting a play table in order to feed a rag doll, only to put it all away to start over again.

Outside work is also enticing to children as young as toddlers. My baby girls loved to follow me or their dad around the garden with a play lawn-mower and would repeatedly bang invisible nails into the floor with a plastic hammer.

Involve children in daily cleaning at a very young age. Keep your babies next to you in an infant seat, in a sling, or in a baby backpack while you make your bed, wipe down the bathrooms, and unload the dishwasher.

Although the temptation is strong to plop the kids in front of a video or shoo them out in the yard, children need to realize from the get-go that daily maintenance is required to keep a household running smoothly.

The clothes do not magically get laundered and returned to their rightful place in the dresser drawer. Someone has spent time and energy to make this happen.

While a three- or four-year-old child will usually eagerly help parents when asked, it may take some gentle persuasion (and sometimes bargaining and coercion!) to entice an older child or teen to help out if they haven't been doing so already.

Monkey See, Monkey Do.

Remember the old adage:

Children learn in 3 ways:

1) By Example

2) By Example

3) By Example

If you come home from work and leave your belongings in a heap by the front door, guess what your child will do? If you never make your bed in the morning, guess what your child will also not do in the morning? If you moan and groan when it is time to tend the garden, guess what your child will do when asked to pull weeds?

On the other hand, if you are reasonably tidy and put away your belongings, your children are much more likely to follow suit.

A nine-month-old baby will happily "clean" toys with a baby wipe if she sees her parents regularly cleaning and dusting.

Perfection Schmerfection

Release the need for perfection when teaching your children to help with the family chores. Your child will not fold the towels as well as you do.

Your child will also take three to four times as long as you do to complete a task—any task.

This is normal. Excruciatingly frustrating, but normal.

Practice your yoga breathing and mentally go to your happy place.

Resist the urge to criticize or "fix" the way your child tidies up. Jumping in too quickly will give a child the impression that he isn't capable of accomplishing the task. An older child (or a spouse!) may begin to sabotage their work in order to get out of daily duties if you routinely come to the rescue.

Remember that any little bit is better than nothing. It's the process and not the product that counts.

The older your child, the more you can expect and the more efficient they will become.

Request a Change

If you have been doing everything for everyone in your family, don't expect your children to suddenly come to the realization that they should be helping.

Sit down together and discuss the things that you and your spouse do on a daily basis to keep the house running and ask for suggestions as how to lighten the load.

Steer the conversation towards family responsibility and how each member needs to do his or her part.

Share a list of chores that you would like help with and age-appropriate jobs each child can adopt to their daily routine. I have provided some suggestions based upon age later in this chapter.

How to Give Effective Directions

When you ask your child to comply with a request, make sure that you have his or her full attention. Turn off distractions from the TV, phone, or video games. If you have a young child, make eye contact and squat down to their level. Your child will instantly tune you out if you tower above them or yell directions from the other side of the house.

Depending on the age of the child and their developmental level, you may be able to give only a one-step direction, but if the play-room is in shambles, telling a child younger than about age 10 to "clean up that room" is completely overwhelming.

Instead, focus on one small piece at a time. Start with what YOU will do and then what you expect your child will do. "I will put the *Lincoln Logs®* away while you put the *Legos®* into this bin."

Hand your child the bin you expect them to use. If you have a very young toddler even this task may seem too burdensome. Try breaking it down even more. "I'm going to put the *Legos* away but I need your help. I'll do the red, blue, and green ones but you are in charge of all of the yellow. Put them into this bin."

AGE-APPROPRIATE CHORES

D o not expect your child to instantly adhere to a list of chores. Monitor closely and always show your child exactly how to perform any new tasks.

9 months-2 years of age

Babies and young toddlers enjoy being "big" helpers and can participate in the following household chores with adult supervision, help, and guidance:

- sort laundry

- empty wastebaskets

- bring in the newspaper

- get the mail

- match socks

- pull up sheet and comforter

- empty the spoons and plasticware from the silverware caddy of the dishwasher

- put toys away in the appropriate container

- "dusting/cleaning" with a baby wipe

3-6 years of age

Preschool-aged children can continue to help with all of the chores listed above, along with the following added responsibilities:

- make own bed

- load/unload dishwasher with assistance

- help younger siblings clean up strewn toys

- feed/water pets

- water plants

- pull weeds

- use a whisk broom to clean up crumbs under dinner table

- use a handheld vacuum cleaner to spot clean, or to vacuum the stairs

- put away own laundry

- set the table for meals

7-10 years of age

School-aged children are capable of fulfilling all of the tasks listed above, as well as these new additions:

-complete an entire load of wash

- help younger siblings put away laundry

- vacuum own room

- maintain order in own room

- sweep kitchen

- load/unload dishwasher independently

- feed the dog/pick up poop in the yard

- clear the table after meals

Pre-teen through teen-aged years

Although teenagers would rather lie around and text all day, they are fully able to help their parents out with most of the housekeeping chores, inside and out, including:

- vacuum house

- sweep house

- clean the refrigerator

- wipe down the bathrooms

- wipe down the kitchen countertops

- help younger siblings as needed

- perform more strenuous work in the garden

This may seem like a lot, but remember that back "in the olden days" children were expected to be productive members of the household.

It is only recently that children have been coddled and protected from strenuous labor, which leaves me to wonder if that is why so many in their early twenties feel overwhelmed when turned "loose" in the world.

Remember that you are not raising children. Hopefully you are raising *future adults.*

By the time children leave for college, they should be able to make a meal, sew on a button, do laundry, mow the lawn, and make dinner for the family.

Rewards and Consequences

Many families successfully use elaborate sticker and reward charts for chores. Some families tie allowance to chores.

My husband and I don't pay or reward our children because we believe this is how things work in a family—everyone does their fair share to keep the house ship-shape and everyone is responsible for their own messes.

If we have a rather large project we are happy to pay for extra help from our children, but we do not dole out or take away money for basic household chores.

That said, you are in charge of your own home. Do whatever works the best for your family and for your particular children.

There are countless natural incentives and consequences that can be applied to the daily tasks. Some tried and true "rules" some families have used successfully are:

- Breakfast will be served after the beds are made.

- Dinner will be served after the table is set.

- Dessert will be served after the dinner dishes are washed or stacked in the dishwasher.

- There will be no clean clothes if you do not sort/wash/put them away.

- Any toys left on the floor of the family room at bedtime will be taken away for ____ days (one day per year of the child's life).

- The tortoise will die if he is not properly fed and watered.

Okay, that last one is a bit harsh, but I'm sure you're getting the idea. But maybe the turtle would be better off living with a family who does remember to feed him regularly?

MAKE CLEANING/ ORGANIZING FUN

Your Friend, The Timer

An inexpensive kitchen timer is the best invention, ever! Children are competitive by nature and love the opportunity to "win." I have already mentioned that I like to schedule 10-Minute-Tidies in our home, but you easily turn this pick up time into a competition.

Set the timer for 10 or 15 minutes for a quick "Pick-Up." Announce that dinner will be served after this quick pick-up and that you will keep track of how quickly the house gets tidied, and that the goal is to better the time each day.

The key to the timer is that it is neutral—it is much easier to comply with the demands of the timer than to Mom's or Dad's nagging requests.

Kid-Safe Cleaning

White vinegar and baking soda are two non-toxic cleansers that you probably already have in the cupboard.

Sprinkle some baking soda on the bottom of the tub or shower for a gentle abrasive cleanser. Allow children to scrub away with a soft brush or sponge. Add some vinegar for a bubbly surprise. Vinegar will also make stubborn bathtub rings vanish.

Fill a spray bottle with 1 cup of water and 2 tablespoons of white vinegar for an effective, safe, and environmentally-friendly glass cleaner. Dress children in swimsuits on a warm day and hand them the trigger-spray bottle filled with homemade cleaner.

Sit back and marvel at how young children will gladly whittle away the hours washing your glass patio doors.

Baby wipes are excellent cleaning rags for children. Let your youngsters wipe away spots on the walls, the dust on tabletops, and mop up spilled juice with these handy disposable cloths.

Don't set your children up for failure. Purchase some child-sized cleaning and gardening tools. Not only is it more efficient, your child will have more fun working with a kid-sized broom and mop.

Mop-Sock Skating

Pour some sudsy water in the middle of the kitchen floor. Instruct your children to put on a pair of old socks (or better yet, some of Daddy's!) and "skate" the floor clean.

This also works well with no water as an (somewhat) efficient way to dust mop.

Fizzing Antacid Tablet Toilet Cleanser

The bubbles from an antacid tablet cleans a toilet bowl surprisingly well. Permit your children to take turns dropping the tablets into the water. Time how long it takes each tablet to dissolve.

Denture-cleaning tablets work for this game, too, and they leave the bowl water tinted blue and smelling minty-fresh.

Wash the Car

Have the kids put on swimsuits, rubber boots and a raincoat. Let them get wet and soapy along with the car.

Toothbrush Clean

Give your child an old toothbrush (child must be old enough to under-stand that this brush can't enter his mouth) and have them scrub the track in the shower or patio sliding door.

Clean with Shaving Cream

Dress children in a swimsuit and plop them into the empty tub or shower enclosure with a can of shaving cream. Children will delight in smear-ing the cream all over the walls and savor the opportunity to write their name or draw pictures in the suds. Hand them scrub-brushes or sponges for a deeper clean. Rinse thoroughly to reveal a squeaky-clean tub or shower.

PLANNING FOR SUCCESS

Family Meeting

I'm a big proponent for family meetings. In Totally Together: Shortcuts to an Organized Life, I list Family Meeting on the To Do list for each week.

It is up to you how to schedule these out, and how big of a deal you want to make about holding meetings. I actually tend to not have them on our family's calendar, but just seize the moment when we are all together to solidify schedules or have a quick conversation about what is happening in the news.

Life is busy—if mealtimes are hectic, don't try to bring up meaningful conversation or a moral dilemma. Every family has different times when they are all together. If sitting down together for dinner is a cherished time, use that as a springboard.

Maybe you are all together on a long drive, or are out to dinner and waiting for your food to arrive. Maybe you have twenty minutes stuck in a theater seat before the show begins.

Don't stress over trying to create a "perfect" scene—it doesn't exist. This is real life. Capture the moment whenever and wherever it presents itself.

Meal Planning

Our family runs better when we have planned meals. Sometimes I go nuts and plan out a month's worth of meals at a time, and other times I am lucky if I know what we're going to eat for dinner by the time I walk through the front door.

Planning meals and snacks is very important if you have food allergies. We happen to be a gluten free family, and have been since 2006. Because of this, it's just not as feasible to ignore meal planning and regular grocery shopping because we can't as easily pick up fast food or a ready-made lasagna to bake at home.

> If you are gluten free, or would like to learn more about cooking and grocery shopping gluten free, you can email me at steph@stephanieodea.com and ask for a free copy of my Going Gluten Free Without Going Crazy ebook and I will send it over to you right away.

Before I had children of my own, I ran preschool centers for the underprivileged. So I *know* how well planning out menus works for little kids. It's the best way to get them to eat "new" things — they just do it because it's written down on the LIST.

and who is to argue with THE LIST?

This does not need to be elaborate in any way shape or form --- this monthly menu can be as simple or as elaborate as you choose to make it.

Since I meal plan and shop for our family of five, I have chosen to stick to "themes" to make my shopping and preparation easier. On Mondays, dinner is usually some sort of pasta or casserole, Tuesdays is chicken, Wednesdays are a "clean out the fridge night" which means we usually have leftover food on top of baked potatoes or rice, Thursdays we have fish, and Fridays in our house is pizza night.

You can do any type of theme you want -- many people have tacos on Tuesday, for example, or they participate in a Meatless Monday. It's your life, your family, and you get to make up the rules! You'll notice that I don't plan out our meals on the weekend. That is because our weekends usually involve eating up leftovers, a restaurant meal, or seeing friends or family.

If you have never planned your family's meals, I urge you to give it a try. I have included in the Appendix a few charts and guides that might be of help that you can photocopy. It stinks to search through an empty fridge and pantry at 5pm with a growling tummy and cranky kids.

Your Friend, The Slow Cooker

When the Crock-Pot® brand introduced the first slow cooker in 1971, it revolutionized the way people create dinner. I never feel so ahead of the game as I do when I plan slow cooker meals and took my love for the slow cooker online when I began my AYearofSlowCooking.com website.

Imagine the satisfaction you feel at 6:30 in the morning from a made-bed multiplied intensely when you also have *dinner* prepared at that time!

I adore my Crock-Pot slow cookers, and have gone so far as toying with the idea of naming them. I have 14 in the house right now and have found a way to cook pretty much anything in them.

If you think that you can only cook meat and potato dishes in a slow cooker, you will be amazed at the different dishes that can be adapted to slow cooking. I have prepared tofu, fish, numerous vegetable dishes, breakfast foods, and even crème brulee, along with adaptations of traditional meat dishes.

Using your slow cooker is also a good way to save money. Inexpensive cuts of meat tenderize nicely during slow-cooking, dried beans soften and cook to perfection, and large quantities can be prepared, and eaten for lunches and subsequent meals.

The slow cooker is also a valuable tool in the hot summer months, because the heat they produce is a fraction of the heat created by using an oven or stovetop. Slow cookers also use less energy than those appliances, and promote cleaner air quality when used to cook instead of an outdoor barbecue.

Housekeepers: Yay or Nay?

I am not anti house cleaners in any way, shape, or form. If you would prefer to have housekeepers come in to do all of the heavy deep cleaning, then I am all for it.

This is your home, and your life.

But if have too much stuff and too much clutter, it's going to be difficult for the house keepers to do their job.

Take some time to P.R.O.M. all of the living spaces of your home so it's super easy to do a 10-Minute-Tidy before they arrive.

If you keep up with the Daily 7 and P.R.O.M. -ing, it should not be an issue to have house keepers come in on a weekly or monthly basis to tackle the deep cleaning and the things you don't want to do yourself.

That said, many readers write to me that they have found a way to "do away" with their long time house keepers once they consistently keep up with the Daily 7.

My friend Sarah told me that after taking the time to P.R.O.M. each kid bedroom and the living room over this past summer, the house was so much easier to clean her family realized they could save the money spent on house keeping and just do it themselves.

To me, having house keepers come in here or there is like having your car detailed.

It's a nicety. Not a necessity.

A necessity is to take the McDonald's wrappers out of your car so it doesn't smell like a French fry factory.

But having someone go over your car with toothpicks and QTips and Armorall the dashboard? NOT A NECESSITY.

A housecleaning service or a housekeeper is a luxury -- and not one I'd begrudge you in any way! But if you are tempted to give it a go on your own (and you must be, if you are reading this book...)

I think you will find that after a few months of sticking to the Daily 7 you will find that your home is cleaner and better maintained than ever before.

Save the housekeeping money for a family vacation or plop it into the 529 accounts!

FINAL NOTES FROM STEPH

T hank you for spending time with me and for picking up this book! I hope you found it helpful and useful.

I write online at StephanieODea.com and at AYearofSlowCooking.com. You are more than welcome to track my down at my websites or on Facebook.

I have a StephanieODea "connection" facebook group where readers can discuss any of my books or cookbooks and ask questions of each other.

You can find that group, here: https://www.facebook.com/groups/odeabookclub

SIMPLE
MEAL PLAN

stephanieodea.com

	MON	TUE	WED	THU	FRI
WEEK 1	B: OATMEAL	B: SCRAMBLED EGGS	B: TOAST	B: FROZEN WAFFLE	B: YOGURT SMOOTHIE
	L: GRILLED CHEESE GRAPES	L: MINI TACOS CARROTS & RANCH	L: CANNED CHILI	L: LUNCH MEAT SANDWICH	L: BEAN BURRITO
	D: LASAGNA	D: CREAMY CHICKEN & RICE	D: SAUSAGE & SWEET POTATOES	D: LEMON SALMON	D: PIZZA
WEEK 2	B: OATMEAL	B: EGGS IN NEST	B: TOAST	B: FROZEN WAFFLE	B: YOGURT SMOOTHIE
	L: LEFTOVERS & FRIED RICE	L: PB & J	L: BEAN BURRITO	L: LUNCH MEAT SANDWICH	L: QUESADILLA
	D: SPAGHETTI & MEAT SAUCE	D: CHICKEN & MASHED POTATOES	D: STIR FRIED VEGETABLES & SAUSAGE	D: PARMESAN TILAPIA	D: PIZZA
WEEK 3	B: OATMEAL	B: VEGGIE OMELETTE	B: TOAST	B: FROZEN WAFFLE	B: YOGURT SMOOTHIE
	L: QUESADILLAS	L: HUMMUS & PITA & VEGGIES	L: MAC & CHEESE	L: CHICKEN FINGERS	L: PB & J
	D: CHICKEN FETTUCINI	D: BAKED LEMON CHICKEN	D: LOADED BAKED POTATOES	D: CAJUN SALMON	D: PIZZA
WEEK 4	B: OATMEAL	B: SCRAMBLED EGGS	B: TOAST	B: FROZEN WAFFLE	B: YOGURT SMOOTHIE
	L: SALAMI & CHEESE	L: GRILLED CHEESE	L: CANNED BAKED BEANS	L: TURKEY & CHEESE ROLLUPS	L: QUESADILLA
	D: PENNE PASTA & SAUSAGE	D: CHICKEN FAJITAS	D: BAKED TOFU AND FRIED RICE	D: BAKED TILAPIA	D: PIZZA

CLEAN LESS PLAY MORE

Stephanie • Dea

DAILY	WEEKLY	TWICE A MONTH	ONCE A MONTH
make beds	vacuum	toothpick clean	dust blinds
laundry	mop kitchen	bathroom deep clean	front porch
garbage cans	kitchen counters	change bedding	polish wood furniture
kitchen sink	clean microwave		clean out car
clean up after self	replace sponge		
bathroom wipe down	speed dust		
10 Minute Tidy			

QUARTERLY		TWICE A YEAR	
	clean out fridge kitchen cabinets windows		smoke detectors flip mattresses HVAC filters

About the Author

Stephanie O'Dea made a new year's resolution to use her slow cooker every single day in 2008 and write about it online. This simple idea resulted in a highly trafficked website and four books, one of which spent six weeks on the New York Times bestseller list.

Stephanie has appeared on Good Morning America (three times) and the Rachael Ray show (four times). She has been featured in Real Simple magazine, Woman's World magazine, and on Oprah.com. She is a contributing editor to Simply Gluten Free magazine and a recipe contributor to ABC.com. She appeared in the Ninja Cooking System infomercial and is a spokesperson for the product. Further information can be found at stephanieodea.com.

LIVE SLOWLY T Shirts now Available!

10 designs in all --- see the collection on Amazon

STEPHANIE O'DEA

Other Books by Stephanie O'Dea

2, 4, 6, EAT:
Intermittent Fasting Simplified

Simple Shortcuts to Peace:
6 Steps to Living the Life of Your Dreams
online course -- email or check facebook group for more info

The Mommy Blogger Next Door:
A.K.A. How I Became The CrockPot Lady

30 Days to A New You:
A Motivational Journal and Workbook

Make It Fast, Cook It Slow:
The Big Book of Everyday Slow Cooking

More Make It Fast, Cook It Slow: 200 Brand-New,
Budget-Friendly, Slow-Cooker Recipes

365 Slow Cooker Suppers

5 Ingredients or Less Slow Cooker Cookbook

Totally Together: Shortcuts to an Organized Life

Slow Cooker Meal Plans

Slow Cooker Recipe Booklets:

Printed in Great Britain
by Amazon

25575443R00047